Short ʲˢʰ Walks
in East Devon

Robert Hesketh

Bossiney Books

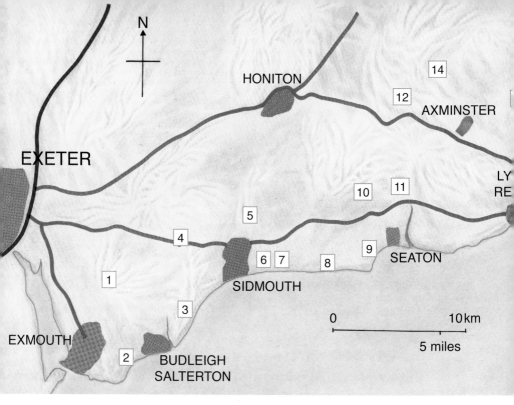

The approximate locations of the walks in this book

All the walks in this book were checked prior to publication, at which time the instructions were correct. However, changes can occur in the countryside over which neither the author nor the publisher has any control. Please let us know if you encounter any serious problems.

This corrected reprint 2013
First published 2006 by
Bossiney Books Ltd, 33 Queens Drive, Ilkley, LS29 9QW
www.bossineybooks.com

© 2006 Robert Hesketh All rights reserved
ISBN 978-1-89938390-0

Acknowledgements
The maps are by Graham Hallowell
Cover based on a design by Heards Design Partnership
The photographs are by the author.

Printed in Great Britain by R Booth Ltd, Penryn, Cornwall

Introduction

This is an invitation to some of England's finest coastal, field and woodland paths, a walker's paradise. High cliffs and pebble-strewn shores, rolling hills cut by sparkling rivers and flower-filled, wooded valleys – East Devon is endlessly enjoyable.

At 4.5 to 10km (3 to 6 miles), the routes in this book can all be walked in a morning or an afternoon. The time you need depends on how fast you walk and how interested you are in what you see.

Safety (please take seriously)

Walking East Devon and its superb coast path is safe and trouble free – if you are prepared. In the first place, the cliff paths are not fenced. Do not go to the edge or beyond any fissures, and follow any signed diversions inland and away from eroded or damaged paths.

Among geologists, East Devon is famed for landslips, which have created spectacular undercliffs, for example Hooken Undercliffs near Beer (Walk 9). Landslips continue to occur frequently. Indeed, 24 diversions to the South West Coast Path were recorded during 2012, the year before this book was revised. So take care.

Secondly, Devon weather can change suddenly. As well as enjoying a generally mild climate, we also know about high winds – and sea mists. It has been known to rain (and *rain*) here too!

Please do not go without good walking boots and suitable clothing. Drinking water, map and compass, plus waterproofs and an extra layer are equally essential, as well as a comfortable rucksack. Many, including me, add a walking stick, mobile phone and food to the list. Please lock your car and don't leave valuables in it.

Ticks are a potential nuisance, especially in hot, humid weather. Wearing long trousers and socks offers some protection against these tiny parasites, which can carry a viral infection, Lyme disease.

Access

The sketch maps in this book are just that – sketches. You should go equipped with the Ordnance Survey Explorers 115 and 116, which cover the area and give information on access too. Please keep to the paths over enclosed farmland, use (and close) gates as appropriate and keep dogs under control, especially near sheep and cliff edges.

I am sure you will enjoy these walks as I have.

Robert Hesketh

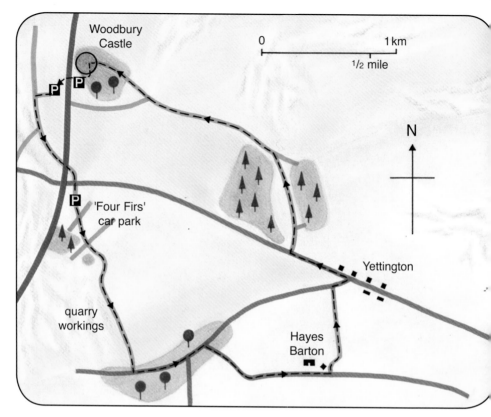

Walk 1   Woodbury Castle and Hayes Barton

Distance: 8.1km (5 miles)   Time: 2¹/₄ hours
Character: This walk over heathland and through woods offers good
views of the coast and the Exe estuary. It passes Sir Walter Ralegh's
birthplace – a handsome Tudor farmhouse – and an impressive
prehistoric hillfort. Some ups and downs, but no strenuous slopes.

Park in the 'Woodbury Castle' car park on the B3180 (SY032872). Take
a quick look at Woodbury Castle, so that you will recognise where you
are on your return. Then cross the road into the 'Estuary' car park opposite, and walk to the far southern end, where an information board
describes the view.

From this board, follow one of the rough paths ahead, downhill to a
broad track, the East Devon Way. Turn left.

Keep to the main track until you reach the road. Cross and take the
narrow path opposite. Cross another road, into the 'Four Firs' car park.
At the far end of the car park, take the path between the signboards.

4

Hayes Barton, where Sir Walter Ralegh was born in 1554

At the fork 60m ahead, bear left. On reaching a line of conifers and a meeting of tracks, walk ahead. Ignore side turnings and stick with the broad stony track, following it downhill then up, with flooded quarry workings on your right. At the top of the rise is a junction of tracks. Continue ahead, dipping then climbing to meet a tarmac lane. Turn left along this lane.

Take the second lane on the right, signed HAYES BARTON. Pass Hayes Barton and after 100m turn left at a gate. This footpath leads via field edges, a stile and a gate to a lane. Turn right, then after 100m turn left along a road (EXETER). After passing the village and speed limit signs, turn right (PUBLIC BRIDLEWAY). After 130m bear left at a fork. Follow the blue waymarks of the bridleway through trees, ignoring side turnings, and continue uphill.

At a T-junction, turn left. Stay on the broad track as it climbs steadily through the heather and furze towards Woodbury Castle, which stands against the horizon, hidden within trees. When the broad track forks, bear right towards the trees. Take a path along the right edge of the wood, then bear left to explore this Iron Age fort, occupied 500-300BC. The car park lies on the left (western) side of the ramparts.

> Woodbury Commons have a stark and sombre quality reminiscent of Hardy's Egdon Heath. Nationally and locally, heathland is an increasingly rare and threatened habitat of great conservation value, and Woodbury Commons are among the largest in England.

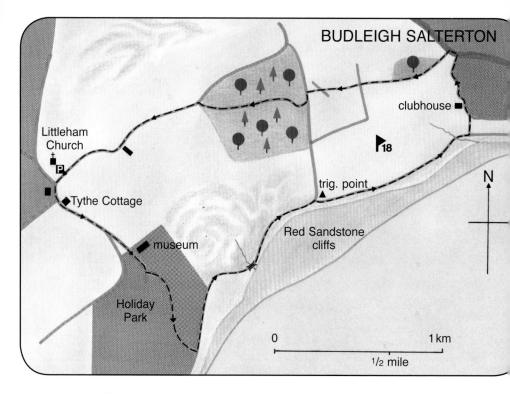

Walk 2   Littleham and West Down

Distance: 6.6km (4 miles)   Time: 2 hours
Character: The cliff-top path offers superb views east along the varied
succession of Devon cliffs, and west to the Exe, Haldon ridge, Dawlish
Warren and Hope's Nose. We return via footpaths and lanes. One
moderate ascent.
   NB Parts of the cliff path are unstable: don't go close to the edge!

Use the parking area by Littleham church. Take the road signed to
SANDY BAY, which curves left at the Clinton Arms and passes thatched
Tythe Cottage. After 600m enter the holiday centre, and when you
reach the lifting barriers bear left (PUBLIC FOOTPATH). Continue on
the same course through the caravan park as signed, to meet the cliff
path. Turn left for COAST PATH.

   Suddenly a spectacular view of West Cliff confronts you, one of
Devon's best examples of fluvial (river-deposited) New Red Sandstone. The coast path climbs steadily to the triangulation pillar on
West Down Beacon, at 129m a superb viewpoint. Ignore the turning
for KNOWLE.

6

Continue on the coast path towards BUDLEIGH SALTERTON, enjoying the views of the town, its pebbly beach, and onward to the mouth of the Otter. Further still stands the succession of New Red Sandstone and chalk cliffs, of such scientific interest that the East Devon/West Dorset coast is Britain's first Natural World Heritage site.

Walk downhill into the trees, cross a streamlet and continue to a coast path waymark. Turn left up a short flight of concrete steps. Walk on to join a lane. Carry straight on, with the golf clubhouse on your left, and follow the lane down to Exmouth Road.

Turn left and almost immediately left again onto LITTLEHAM CHURCH PATH. Follow this well-beaten path through trees. Ignore a cross path, then skirt the edge of the golf course – beware golf balls! The path continues along the edge of a field then crosses another part of the course. Entering trees, turn left at the footpath sign, and almost immediately right, LITTLEHAM CHURCH PATH.

Follow the path through Knowle Hill Plantations to reach a lane. Turn left and walk back to Littleham's mainly 15th century church. Admiral Nelson's widow is buried in the churchyard. The church has a good rood screen and parclose screens and some 15th century glass.

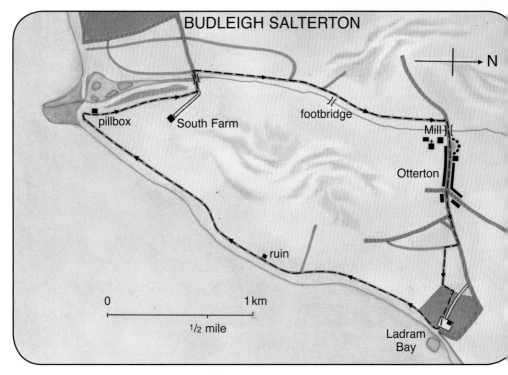

Walk 3   Otterton and Ladram Bay

Distance: 9.75 km (6 miles)   Time: 2¹/₄ hours
Character: Superb views of the Jurassic Coast, and bird-watching on the
Otter Estuary Nature Reserve. Otterton has a street of cob and thatch
houses, and a working water-mill. Easy walking, no really steep slopes.
*   NB Take binoculars.*

Park with care at Otterton's green, just east of the mill. Walk past the King's Arms, beside the stream along Fore Street. The massive chimneystacks (some dated) in the side walls of these 16th and 17th century cottages and farmhouses are typical of Devon. When the road bends left, walk ahead up BELL STREET LEADING TO LADRAM BAY.

   Continue uphill. Ignore the tarmac lanes on the right, then near the top of the slope turn right along an unsigned track. Just 35 m ahead, turn left down a track, again signed LADRAM BAY.

   The track becomes a path and emerges into the Ladram Bay holiday centre. Continue ahead, signed COAST PATH, then keep right for BUDLEIGH SALTERTON.

   You will get an arresting view of Ladram Bay's rock stacks. These are part of a chain of New Red Sandstones, between 180 and 225 million

8

years old, that stretch from Torbay to east of Sidmouth. High Peak stands behind the stacks and on a clear day the view extends along the Dorset coast to Portland Bill. Follow the undulating cliff path for 4km to the River Otter. Seabirds, especially gulls, wheel and call below. They find nesting sites along ledges and crevices. Don't go too close to the edge – it's a sheer drop.

Follow the coast path when it turns inland at a WW2 pillbox, now maintained as a winter bat roost. There are bat-boxes in the trees along the river bank, where a hide offers excellent opportunities to watch birds. They are plentiful throughout the year, but especially in winter, when waders gather.

In medieval times, before the shingle ridge formed and silt built up, the Otter was navigable to Otterton. The saltpans of Budleigh Salterton were worked where now there are mudflats.

Turn left onto a lane at South Farm. Keep left to cross a bridge and turn right on the bankside footpath to OTTERTON. Watch out for fish, including trout and mullet, and birds including kingfishers.

Continue on the same bank, passing a metal bridge. When you reach a road, turn right across the bridge past Otterton Mill. The Domesday Book records three mills at Otterton, including one on this site. It still grinds flour. You may like to study the restored machinery in motion, and visit the gallery and craft workshops.

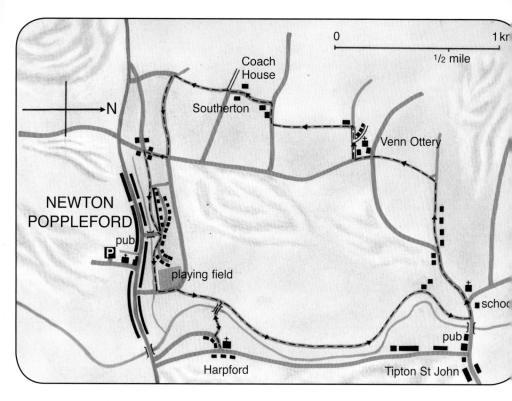

Walk 4 Newton Poppleford

Distance: 7.8 km (4³/₄ miles) Time: 2¹/₂ hours
Character: A gentle, largely level walk, with pleasant views of pastoral
East Devon. It follows the banks of the Otter then returns by quiet lanes
and footpaths.

From the car park behind the church at Newton Poppleford, take the
path down beside the tower. Cross the A3052 at the traffic lights and
turn left, then take the first right, MEADOW DRIVE. Turn right into
CHESTNUT WAY, then bear right on the tarmac footpath beside the
stream. Follow it past playing fields, then turn left along a lane as far
as the first bend.

Turn right onto the footpath and continue to the riverbank. Cross
the Otter by a metal bridge to visit Harpford with its cob and thatch
houses. Retrace your steps across the bridge and turn right, following
the bankside path upstream to Tipton St John.

If you need refreshment, the Golden Lion lies 200m to your right.
Otherwise, turn left. Walk to St John's Church (1840 and noted for its
stained glass) and take the lane to the left (VENN OTTERY). After 350m

10

Harpford church, where the churchyard cross has a memorial to Augustus Toplady, author of 'Rock of Ages' and vicar of Harpford

when the lane turns sharp left, go straight ahead (UNSUITABLE FOR MOTORS) and walk up the track for 400m.

Turn left onto a track, distinguished by a fenced triangle of bushes. At a road junction, go forward on the lane to NEWTON POPPLEFORD but after 100m turn right (UNMETALLED ROAD). After 150m turn right across grass to visit Venn Ottery church, then return to the track and turn right along it, passing new houses to your right, then turning left uphill across the front of an older house.

On reaching a lane, turn right, then left after 150m. Bear right at the post box ahead and follow the lane as it curves left and uphill. Pass the Coach House and Southerton Park. When the lane curves sharp left, take the footpath straight ahead. This enters a field by steps and a stile. Continue up an enclosed path to a small metal gate. Follow the footpath left. Turn left into the lane, which leads downhill and gives a good view of Newton Poppleford.

At the road junction turn right, then after 100m turn left and left again into a PUBLIC FOOTPATH. After two fields this passes the backs of houses and returns you to MEADOW DRIVE. Turn right and retrace your steps to the start.

> Newton Poppleford was built as a medieval new town and granted a market in 1226. Although often disguised by later facades, many of the cottages in the main street are very old, especially those east of the Exeter Inn, which itself began life as a medieval church house.

11

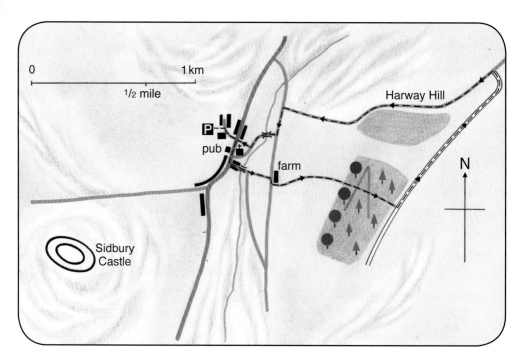

Walk 5 Sidbury

Distance: 5.3km (3 1/4 miles)   Time: 1 1/2 hours
*Character: Sidbury has cob and thatch cottages and a medieval church
with a Norman tower. A steep climb and a fairly steep descent (on
tarmac, so it could be dangerous in icy conditions) yield splendid views
over the rolling hills and deep valleys. Footpath, track and a quiet lane.*

From the car park behind Sidbury's Parish Room (SY139919), turn
right and right again into the main street. Just past the Red Lion and
the church, turn left down BRIDGE STREET. Cross the bridge on the
EAST DEVON WAY, and climb a steep lane.

Turn right at a T-junction and after only 30m go through a gate
on the left. Keep the field edge on your right, then turn right through
a gate. Continue with the hedge on your left, but stop to admire the
view, including Sidbury Castle, an Iron Age hillfort which gave the
village its name.

Cross a stile and continue straight up the slope (crops permitting)
to enter the woodland via a small bridge. The path begins to rise much
more steeply through the trees, cutting straight across two woodland
tracks.

On reaching the summit at 195 m, continue in the same direction for 200 m, then turn left along a broad track (EAST DEVON WAY). On your right is Harcombe, a steep wooded valley or combe, so typical of Devon. The name means 'hare combe' and Harecombe Farm was recorded in 1200.

After 1 km the track reaches a lane – Harway Hill. Turn left here and enjoy the views of the Sid valley as you descend steeply to a road junction. Turn left, then take the first lane on the right down to the church, noted for its 7th century crypt. A short flight of steps leads to the right of the churchyard and out to the main street. Turn right and retrace your steps back to the start.

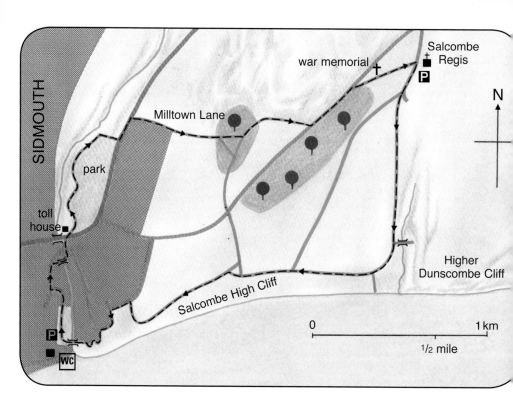

Walk 6 Salcombe Regis and Sidmouth

Distance: 6.7km (4¹/₄ miles) Time: 2¹/₂ hours
Character: This fairly demanding walk offers excellent coastal views
with dramatic cliffs, as well as beautiful farmland and woods. Allow for
two stiff ascents and two steep descents. Could be combined with Walk 7.

Start from the church car park in Salcombe Regis, SY148888 (contributions requested). Turn left and follow the lane downhill.

Ignore the footpath TO SOUTH COMBE FARM but 30m further on take PUBLIC FOOTPATH SALCOMBE MOUTH through a kissing gate on the right.

Bear right through another gate (yellow waymark) and follow a well-beaten path to meet the coast path at a footbridge. Keep right for SIDMOUTH.

Pause on the steep path up Salcombe High Cliff for a fine view of Higher Dunscombe behind you, rising to 156m. Steps aid the final part of the ascent, and there are benches with inviting views!

The descent towards Sidmouth starts steeply, with a grand vista of

14

The view westward from Salcombe Hill Cliff, looking over the town of Sidmouth and towards High Peak

cliffs stretching westwards. It becomes gentler as we approach this most genteel resort. Follow COAST PATH signs and acorn waymarks as the path turns briefly inland, then left down lanes and then a tarmac path down to Alma Bridge – where there is access to the shingle beach. Cross the Sid and follow the path up the west bank through a play park, then slightly to the left following back streets parallel to the river. Recross the Sid by a footbridge next to a ford. With the river to your left, walk on past the toll house (1817) to enter a park.

Still keeping the river, with its pretty waterfalls, on your left, walk through the park. Turn right at the sign SALCOMBE HILL VIA MILLTOWN LANE. Turn left onto the main road and after 130m turn right up MILL-TOWN LANE. Climbing steadily, the lane becomes a track.

On reaching a wood, keep left and climb more steeply up steps. At the top of the steps, turn left and continue uphill past an avenue of beeches. Ignore side turnings and continue to a lane. Turn left, then bear right at the war memorial, down to the church and car park.

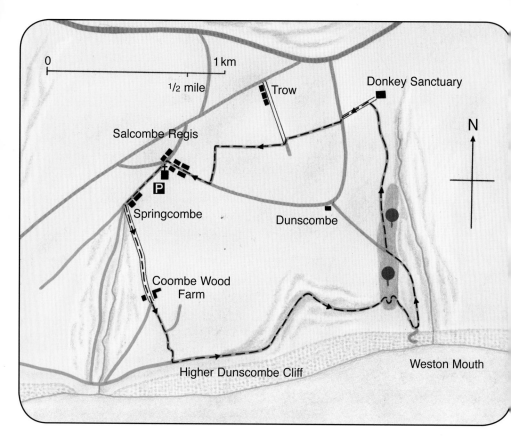

Walk 7 Salcombe Regis and Weston Mouth

Distance: 5.6km (3¹/2 miles) Time: 2 hours
Character: This beautiful cliff top walk offers splendid views of the
Jurassic Coast, but calls for a stiff climb up and down. It is linked by
quiet paths, rich with wild flowers in Spring. On the way are a donkey
sanctuary and a handsome church. Could be combined with Walk 6.

Turn left out of the church car park at Salcombe Regis (SY148888).
Follow the lane downhill. Keep left at Springcombe and follow the tarmac ahead to COMBE WOOD FARM. Continue past the thatched farmhouse to a metal gate. Bear left and climb steadily uphill on a broad
footpath until it curves sharp left. Continue ahead here on a narrower
path. It leads out to a junction with the coast path.

Turn left and follow the coast path along Higher Dunscombe and
then inland to the top of Lincombe. Follow the path right, along the
cliff-top, and then steeply down towards Weston Mouth. Ignore the

16

path on your left signed DUNSCOMBE. Ahead of you is Weston Cliff, its red sandstone base capped by a beautiful creamy rock, Greensand. This used to be quarried nearby, and the quarries were reopened in 1979 for Exeter cathedral's restoration programme.

You will reach a T-junction. Unless you fancy a bathe (remembering that Weston is a nudist beach, and also that the steeply shelving shingle makes leaving the water difficult) turn left for DUNSCOMBE.

Fork right at the next path junction (SLADE HOUSE FARM DONKEY SANCTUARY) along a path carpeted with bluebells in May.

Turn left into the Sanctuary (PUBLIC FOOTPATH SALCOMBE REGIS) and then keep left on the footpath to a lane. (Alternatively, buy a ticket and spend some time here. It is run primarily as a charity rather than a tourist attraction.)

Cross the lane and continue on the footpath TROW AND SALCOMBE REGIS. At the next junction the signs are confusing. Ignore the finger-post. Turn left across the stile, then right through two gates. Continue ahead along the enclosed path, crossing two stiles.

Cut diagonally left, following the faint path across the field to a stile. Cross and turn right onto a lane. Follow it downhill past thatched cottages to a junction. Turn left here for the church and car park.

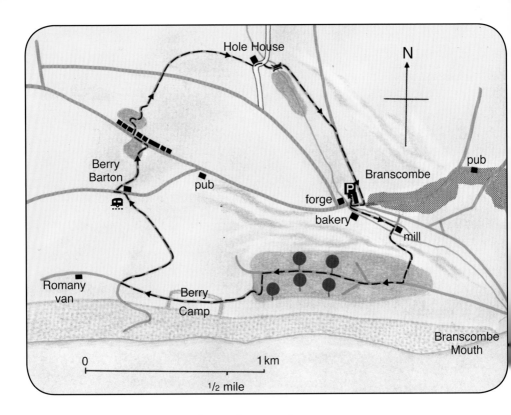

Walk 8 Branscombe and Berry Camp

Distance: 5.8km (3³/₄ miles)   Time: 2 hours
Character: From Branscombe, with its thatched forge, restored bakery
and working watermill, we climb to Berry Camp, an ancient
fortification offering splendid coastal views. The return is by quiet field
and woodland paths, involving some uneven ground and one very
muddy patch near the end of the walk.

Park at Branscombe Village Hall (voluntary donations please) and
watch the smiths at work in the unique forge. Cross the road and go
through a gate.

Follow the footpath past Devon's last traditional bakery. The baking
equipment is preserved and teas are available.

Walk ahead, FOOTPATH TO MILL. At the mill, turn sharp right up a
steep track. Continue steeply uphill as signed by yellow waymarks to a
stile and then on up steps. Turn right at the acorn-signed waymark and
walk through the woods.

18

After 700 m, turn left for WESTON MOUTH. At the next signpost turn right and climb up to Berry Camp, a large earth-banked fort, probably Iron Age. Its seaward side is being lost in cliff falls. Continue on the coast path to a coast path waymark offering alternative routes. Turn sharp right, almost doubling back, BERRY BARTON.

This takes you into a field where you head for a gate with very light-coloured stone surrounds. Turn left onto the PUBLIC FOOTPATH.

At the lane by Berry Barton, turn left again. After 80 m, turn right onto the PUBLIC FOOTPATH which runs behind the farm. Turn left at the end of the second field, and keep the hedge on your right. Cross a stile, and follow the woodland path steeply downhill to a lane.

Turn left. Only 100 m ahead, turn right between houses into a PUBLIC FOOTPATH which climbs to a field. Follow the field edge right then left to a stile. Cross, turn left, and cross two more stiles to a lane. Take the bridleway ahead to HOLE HOUSE.

Turn left past the front of Hole House and downhill. Turn right over a stile onto a PUBLIC FOOTPATH. It leads down to duckboards and a stream. This part can be very muddy! Cross the footbridge and follow the path downstream. It gradually rises to meet a lane. Turn right and follow the lane downhill to the village.

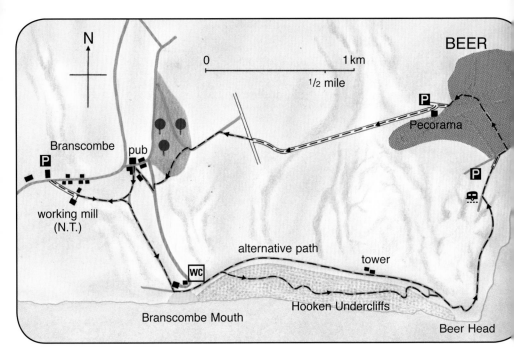

Walk 9   Branscombe and Beer

Distance: 8.8km (5¹/₂ miles)   Time: 2¹/₂ hours
Character: An exhilarating coastal walk to Beer Head, England's most westerly chalk cliff, with views of the Heritage Coast from Torbay to Portland Bill, and exploring the remarkable landslip of the Hooken Undercliffs. Two steep ascents and uneven walking through the Undercliffs.

Park at Branscombe Village Hall car park (SY 197888, voluntary contributions please) near the unique thatched forge, open to the public (National Trust). Turn left out of the car park, then after 40m turn right (BRANSCOMBE MOUTH). Follow the leat to the mill entrance then continue ahead for BRANSCOMBE MOUTH. Keep right at the next junction and walk down to the beach, with its shop, café and toilets.

Turn left and follow the coast path up East Cliff. Halfway up there's a choice of paths. Despite the initial climb, the upper route is easier, but the lower route through the Undercliffs is a unique experience.

Hooken Undercliffs were formed in one night in 1790. Four hectares of land slipped 60m down and moved 200m seaward. Heavy rain made the top layer of Upper Chalk and Greensand slip over the layer of clay which separated it from the underlying Lias. Vegetation has since clothed many of the scars, but pinnacles of rock stand up proud.

20

When you reach a path junction, turn right (though you might want to turn briefly left, to take a look at the landslip from above). Follow the coast path to a tarred lane. Turn right at a No Entry sign into COMMON LANE and after 30m left into a footpath behind houses. Cross a lane and continue on the footpath.

Cross another lane, and head diagonally left up a footpath. Turn left onto a road, then after 80m turn right for PECORAMA AND PLEASURE GARDENS. Ascend past the entrance to Pecorama.

At the entrance to the car park turn left onto PUBLIC FOOTPATH-BRANSCOMBE. Now walk for 1.4km to a track T-junction, and continue ahead on a footpath across a field. Go through another kissing gate and turn right, then almost immediately left, keeping the hedge on your right.

When you reach a stile, turn right into the wood, then turn left downhill into BRANSCOMBE, ignoring side turnings. Turn left onto a lane, then after 30m turn sharp right down to the medieval Mason's Arms with its period photographs, open fires and beer garden. Retrace your steps to the crossroads and turn right (BRANSCOMBE MOUTH). Turn right at the path junction and return to the Village Hall.

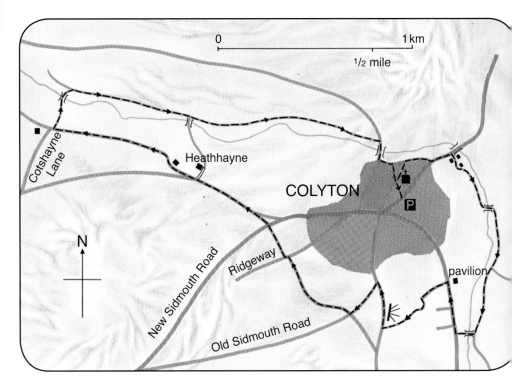

Walk 10 Around Colyton

Distance: 6.6 km (4 miles)   Time: 2 hours
Character: Set amid green hills by the River Coly, historic Colyton is
a gem, with many fine buildings. The walk follows a beautiful river-
bank path and quiet lanes, offering several good viewpoints. One short,
sharp, ascent. One short stretch can be very muddy indeed after rain.

Start from the Dolphin Street car park. Walk ahead across the town
square, by Old Church House (1612), and take the footpath between
Vicarage Street and the churchyard.

   At the end of the footpath turn left and almost immediately bear
right at the Gerard Arms (signed TRAMWAY). Immediately before the
bridge turn right (signed PUBLIC FOOTPATH and with a pink East Devon
Way sign). Follow the footpath around buildings and then follow the
riverbank to Ham Bridge.

   Cross this footbridge and follow the opposite bank downstream. Do
not divert left. Continue to the next footbridge, cross and turn right
along the pavement. Walk on for 250 m. Opposite a pavilion, turn left
and walk up NEWBERY CLOSE. At the top, follow the PUBLIC FOOTPATH

22

Right: The 15th century octagonal tower of St Andrew's, Colyton, is a landmark for miles around

Wet weather diversion: The main route can become very muddy at its western end. An alternative is to turn right at Heathhayne Cross into the bridleway for HEATHHAYNE FARM, *a stone and thatch farmhouse of considerable age. Follow the bridleway to the riverbank and, 100m ahead, cross the Coly by the footbridge and turn right.*

around the houses, then uphill through a field. At the top of the slope, turn right along the lane. On your right there is a viewpoint with a helpful viewing table.

Walk along the lane to the next junction and turn left, uphill. Take the next turning right, along a narrow lane, then walk ahead across RIDGEWAY LANE and then across another lane at 'Little Acre'. The lane forks at Heathhayne Cross. Bear right. Except after heavy rain, continue along the lane from Heathhayne Cross for 750m.

Just before reaching the thatched house at Cotshayne Lane, turn right at a metal field-gate. There is no footpath sign.

Walk past a ruined barn and down through a field. This section can be very muddy after heavy rain. Cross the River Coly by a footbridge. Turn right and follow the East Devon Way downriver for 2km.

On reaching the three-arched stone bridge in Colyton, turn right. Take the first left, VICARAGE STREET, and follow it to the square, then retrace your steps to the car park.

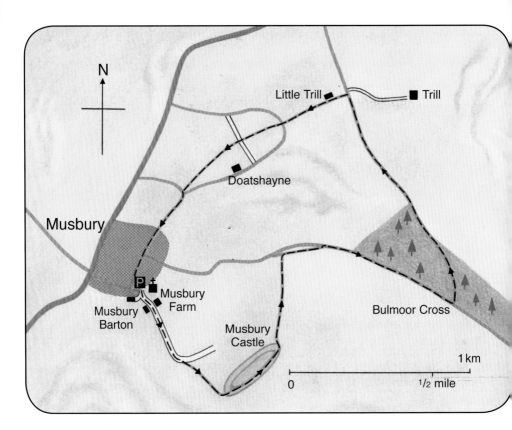

Walk 11   Musbury

Distance: 6km (3³/₄ miles)   Time: 1³/₄ hours
Character: Choose a clear day. The steep climb at the start is rewarded
with marvellous views from Musbury Castle, one of a string of Iron Age
hillforts guarding the high ridges of East Devon. South lie the sea and
Beer Head. Eastward the views stretch into Dorset, north and west over
the Axe Valley and into Somerset. It must have been a strong defensive
position. About half the walk is on lanes, but they are very quiet ones.

Turn left out of the church car park (ST 275946). Bear right opposite
the school into MUSBURY BARTON, then follow the track left uphill via
MUSBURY FARM. After 350 m, cross a stile on the right (PUBLIC FOOT-
PATH). Continue uphill through a field and cross another stile.

After 100 m, where the East Devon Way bears off right and downhill, instead continue ahead and uphill on a well-beaten path.

You will soon reach the discernible rampart of Musbury Castle. This
would have been a hard uphill slog for anyone foolish enough to attack

Seaton and Beer Head, seen from Musbury Castle

under a hail of spears, stones and arrows. Turn left and follow the path along the line of this rampart. The most impressive ramparts are another 350 m further on.

Leave the fort by a stile and follow the waymark left to another stile. Turn right and follow the ridge, with the hedge on your right. Cross another stile. At the end of the field, cross the stile on the right and walk up to the lane.

Turn right and walk for 800 m to Bulmoor Cross. Turn left for TRILL. Follow the lane for 1.3 km to a road junction. Turn left, past Little Trill. At a fork in the lane, take the PUBLIC FOOTPATH ahead, between the two lanes. Cut diagonally across the field to a stile. Cross a track and a second stile, then continue in the same direction along field edges with further stiles.

Emerging onto a lane, turn left and follow it as it curves right. Walk straight on to return to the starting point. The church is noted for its 15th century tower and Drake monument.

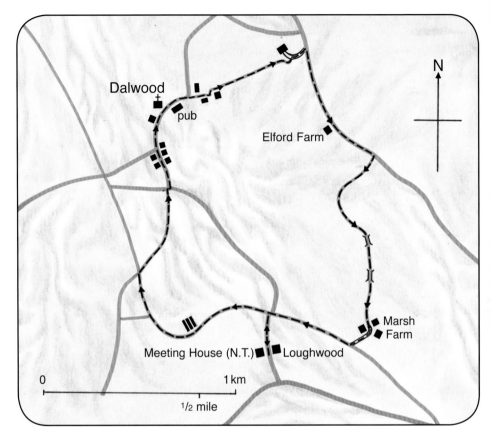

Walk 12 Dalwood

Distance: 5.5km (3½ miles)   Time: 1¾ hours
Character: Footpaths and quiet lanes. One stiff ascent is rewarded with
fine views north towards the Blackdowns. En route is a 17th century
Baptist chapel and a medieval inn. Dalwood means 'dale wood'. Most
of the trees have long gone, but the village shelters comfortably in its
dale or valley.

Use the parking space by the church (ST 2480056). Walk down past
the 12th century Tucker's Arms – which has flagged floors, exposed
beams and a cavernous fireplace. Continue over the bridge. When the
road turns left, take the footpath straight on. Walk uphill past the bun-
galow, go through a metal gate on the left, then continue uphill via two
stiles to a cottage. Walk up the drive to the lane, and turn right.

  Walk past Elford Farm, with its large, typically West Country, 'lat-
eral' chimneystack (built out from a side-wall, rather than internally

26

or on an end wall). Ignore the bridleway by the farm, and continue on the lane for a further 250 m.

Turn right over a stile and down steps. Go through a metal gate and follow the rough track downhill. Where it ends, cut diagonally left across the field (150° or roughly SSE if you have a compass) to the first metal gate on the left. Follow the same line across the next field to a small footbridge, half hidden in the hedge. Continue across the next field, slightly to the left (due south) and cross a footbridge.

Walk to Marsh Farm and through the yard. Follow the concrete track to the lane and turn right. Take the next lane on the left and walk uphill to Loughwood Meeting House (National Trust, admission free), with its thatched roof and rubble walls. Dating from the mid-17th century, it was built in this secluded spot to avoid harassment by the authorities. The box pews are early 19th century.

Retrace your steps to the staggered crossroads and turn left. Continue for 1 km to SUNNYLANDS CROSS. Take the PUBLIC FOOTPATH on the right at a small wooden gate. Walk across the middle of the field and through a metal gate. Turn left and cross two fields by gates. Turn right onto a lane, and almost immediately left. Follow this lane past houses to a junction, and turn right back to the church and/or pub.

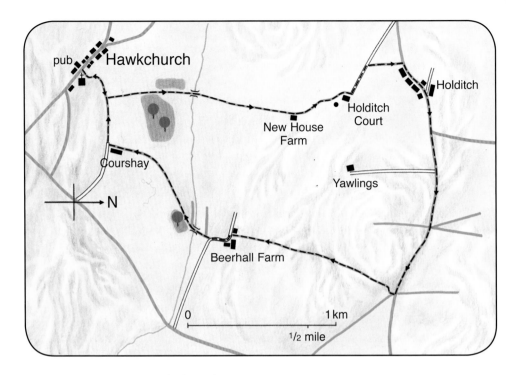

Walk 13 Hawkchurch

Distance: 7.3 km (4¹/₂ miles) Time: 2¹/₄ hours
Character: An exploration of the hilly country on the Dorset border,
this walk offers grand views. It has ups and downs but no very long or
steep slopes. Hawkchurch has a splendid old inn with a carriage arch
and the church retains beautiful Norman arches and carved capitals.

Park opposite the church (ST 343004) or in the pub car park – but please ask first. Take the PUBLIC FOOTPATH through the churchyard and beyond. At the junction of paths, turn left down the bridleway. 500 m ahead, go through two metal gates, ignore the footpath to the right and carry straight on with the hedge on your left. Follow the bridle-way downhill, through a gate and over a footbridge.

You have now crossed the Blackwater into Dorset. Walk uphill on the bridleway, just left of thatched New House Farm. Follow the track uphill and round to the left of Holditch Court, with its curious ruined tower. Bear left onto a tarred farm track. Take the next stile on the right and follow the footpath across the field, to a point about 50 m left of the thatched cottage. Turn right onto the lane and walk past Holditch, which has several attractive buildings including Manor Farm.

When the lane curves left, continue ahead (HOLDITCH HALL). Pass the entrance to Yawlings. Ignore the first bridleway on the right. The next sign indicates a footpath from the left and a footpath to the right. Turn right off the road and immediately right through a gate, and cut diagonally right as signed across the field to a stile. Continue with the hedge on your left. At the bottom of the field, take a stile to the left and continue in the same direction. Cross a field to a water trough.

Now head towards the farm, pass a large green silo to your left and follow the farm track downhill. When it veers left, carry on along a footpath to cross a bridge – back into Devon.

Continue up a track with a small wood on your left. Go through a gate (MONARCH'S WAY) and take the direction shown by the waymark. Pass to the right of houses, go through a kissing gate and turn right along the track. Go through a field gate and follow the path. At a junction, turn left back to the church and pub.

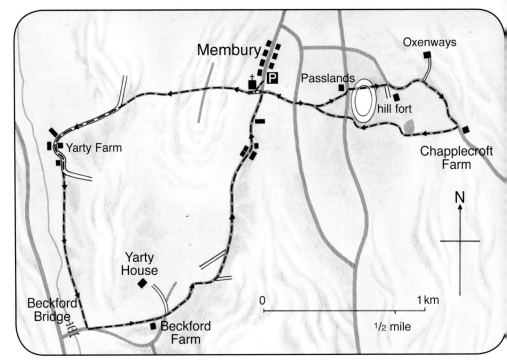

Walk 14 Membury

Distance: 7.7km (4³/₄ miles)   Time: 2¹/₂ hours
Character: A figure-of-eight walk in attractive hilly country. The first
loop is 5.1km and includes a packhorse bridge, the second, visiting the
Iron Age hillfort that gave Membury its name, is 2.6km.

From the free car park (ST 277030) turn left into the PUBLIC BRIDLEWAY
in front of the village hall. Bear right up the lane past Membury's beautiful church – noticing the gargoyles as you pass. After 350m turn left
at a T-junction and almost immediately right on a PUBLIC FOOTPATH.
Follow this with the hedge on your left, and on through a gate.

Continue downhill, joining a concrete track which twists down to
Yarty Farm. Follow it to the left of the farm. When the track turns
sharp left, go forward through a metal gate. Cut diagonally across a
field to another metal gate at the far right, then diagonally again across
another field to a stile at the far right.

Continue parallel to the River Yarty through fields to a lane. Beck-
ford Bridge, on your right, is characteristic of the packhorse era, before carts and waggons became common in Devon at the very end of
the 18th century. Turn left up the lane and take the PUBLIC FOOTPATH
on the left after 35m. Keep to the left of the house ahead of you.

30

When you reach the tarmac lane, continue ahead up it, ignoring side paths, and follow it as it curves left (MEMBURY), which will take you past some handsome cottages back to the church. Either continue a few metres to the car park, or turn right up the steep lane opposite the church for the second loop. At the top of the lane, take the PUBLIC FOOTPATH up steps and over a stile. Cross the field to another stile and a junction of paths. Walk ahead and slightly left towards the thatched farmhouse, Passlands.

Turn left onto the lane, then turn right through a gate opposite Passlands. Climb to another gate and into Membury Castle. The outer rampart of this Iron Age hillfort is clearly visible. Leave by the stile opposite and descend to a lane.

Continue straight ahead and downhill past the entrance to Oxenways. About 20 m before Chapplecroft Farm, turn right through a gate. Follow the PUBLIC FOOTPATH uphill, aiming to circle round the left corner of the copse. Turn right through a metal gate, then press on uphill with the hedge on your left to a stile. Continue uphill, and bear right (ignoring a garden gate ahead of you) to skirt the edge of the fort.

Cross the lane ahead via two stiles and cut diagonally right across the field, to the path junction you passed earlier. Retrace your steps downhill towards the church and car park.

Some other Bossiney walks books

Shortish walks in north Devon (5-8 km walks)
Shortish walks on Dartmoor (5-8 km walks)
Shortish walks near Exeter (4-9 km walks)
Shortish walks on Exmoor (5-9 km walks)
Shortish walks Lower Tamar Valley (6-8 km walks)
Shortish walks – The south Devon coast (6-10 km walks)
Shortish walks – Torbay and Dartmouth (5-8 km walks)

Really short walks South Dartmoor (3-5 km walks)
Really short walks East Devon coast (3-6 km walks)
Really short walks Exmoor and Brendon (3-6 km walks)
Really short walks North Devon (3-5 km walks)
Really short walks South Devon (3-5 km walks)

North Dartmoor pub walks (7-13 km walks)
South Dartmoor pub walks (7-13 km walks)
North Devon pub walks (8-18 km walks)
Exmoor pub walks (8-15 km walks)
Walks on High Dartmoor (7-20 km walks)